Sleepers' Republic

Sleepers' Republic

David Gruber

Astrophil Press
2008

Copyright © 2008 by David Gruber
Cover photograph by Sarah Sonner
Author photograph by Luke Strosnider
Layout and design by duncan b. barlow

Astrophil Press
2008

Library of Congress Cataloging-in-Publication Data
Gruber, David, 1978
  Sleepers' Republic/David Gruber
        p. cm.
  ISBN 0-9822252-0-2 (pbk. : alk.paper)
  1. Poetry
Library of Congress Control Number: 2008941122

http://www.astrophilpress.com

For my parents

Acknowledgements

Poems from this collection have appeared, usually in somewhat different form, in the chapbooks *If By Sea* (Tempest Books, 2006) and *Distant Invasions* (Less Press, 2008), as well as these journals: *The American Drivel Review*, *Columbia: A Journal of Literature and Art*, *Copper Nickel*, *Denver Quarterly*, *Elimae*, *The Furnace Review*, and *Matter*.

Thanks are due to: Ryan Murphy, Christian TeBordo, and Duncan Barlow for taking a chance on publishing my work; Erik Anderson for editing this collection; Bin Ramke, Brian Kiteley, and Clark Davis, each of whom contributed to making the book better; Mekeel McBride and Robert Kelly, who taught me so much; Andrea Berger, Seth Boyd, and Jessica Starr, who, over the years, have given me help with these poems well beyond the ordinary requirements of friendship.

Table of Contents

I

II

III

And when they run over a man that is walking in his sleep, a supernumerary sleeper in the wrong position, and wake him up, they suddenly stop the cars, and make a hue and cry about it, as if this were an exception. I am glad to know that it takes a gang of men for every five miles to keep the sleepers down and level in their beds as it is, for this is a sign that they may sometime get up again.

— Henry David Thoreau, *Walden*

The sleeper is the proprietor of an unknown land. He goes about another business in the dark — and we, his partners, who go to the opera, who listen to gossip of café friends, who walk along the boulevards, or sew a quiet seam, cannot afford an inch of it; because, though we would purchase it with blood, it has no counter and no till.

— Djuna Barnes, *Nightwood*

I

Biedermeier

And turning towards night
whispers reports of failures and losses
from the front that blacken
all the playful beaches hot
with nude whispers continually

walking long streets
distant invasions awake

Approved Methods

Strange wedding music, savage
echo against the brass door
a coughing
an interruption
that slid through the water
where we hung.

I sang a begging tune
and you touched my hand
with the burning plate.

Hushed
a breath drawn
a twist to the fingers.

We swam as in a dream
mediocre against the ruins
bold still, claiming, still gold in memory.
Mouthed secrets to each other
that we were surprised
to discover we kept, I stared
at your bare breast,
shining with reflected light.
A pink beacon drawing us
towards shore,
a new haven in giving freely of
invented intelligence –

We nod at our ancestors
standing for the recessional;
remnants of empire
sing back to us as we drift
alive once more but
without a guide
by which to know each other.

Transport

I had been that ghost wavering
on a footbridge. They cut off my head
once they broke my neck once
once they pulled my arms
tender from their sockets.

                    I gulped down my last breaths
which were epistles addressed to you
from the trash-strewn foot of the gallows.

I soiled my pants going up that ladder.

After, I dreamed of being in your belly
when they split it open and emerging
fully-grown and blood-slick,
swinging my son by his hair,
                        flesh to bludgeon flesh,

blowing steam from my nose and ateeter
at the edge of the earth a new heaven of stars
spread open above me as the body of a woman, the body of a child:

as we are folded in our blankets,
                  as we are rebels.

Knights of the Holy Ghost, or, De Quirós at Santa Cruz

Still crouch the heavy lifters, the yellow
mandibles with which we'd build a future,
with which we tie ourselves like a suture
to each other, to make a thing from fallow
earth, though the lake at first was a shallow
from whence we drew the water to ensure
our concrete would be thick, our structure pure.
Our materials were mixed, men to follow.

Then we received your bent postcard, the news
that you had spanned two lands together, that
you stood for us on the edge of the world
and gathered up the most pitiful truths;
I took up my tools and went home, and sat
and watched as the plan unlaced, unfurled.

If By Sea

These sorrows become us –
that with one breath we will return to the shops
that we will hold in our hands
all the delights from kitchens
far beyond our franchise.

We trot between magnificent and
general states swamped by a yellow,
by a glow that drowns within
our wombs plumped
by certain unbearable expressions,
the new face pressed to the glass:

down with the kings and the lawyers,
the shopkeeper with golden nails.

Just before we expected the turnabout
there was a sudden fit of pique
and the principals found themselves
lying beneath a starry field
hugging black bombs close to its black breast.

As a child, I was friends with
the music of a tin spoon upon a milk jug,
the wide-awake corpse huddled between
rye and rye making our faces sweat.

Soon the chopping will reach our native oaks.
We must say goodbye here
before centuries wash our faces
clean off this slate.
                        The train is firmly behind us,
taking our laughing brothers and sisters
to the family graveyard. If you send to me
your best name, I promise
to wrap it to my guts,
to see it spilled over the merest slight.

Das Kapital

Just what you expected:
photographs with subject at the image's center,
catching the best side, always.

Bright at the heart of each affliction
is a jigsaw missing one piece
and it is an ordeal to sort the volcano
from the weeds:
the one-time sale, the one true reproduction.
You have paid for it in full,
this sport, yet still owe.

It is in there somewhere.
We have been chosen; we wait.

In the morning, if you are lucky,
you shit. And it is a great relief.

First Among Equals

What we like about you is the way
you keep your smirk inside.
Your French cuffs. Your children and
their snowman, his head listing
to one side and no arms.
How you scorn the night like you scorn
a child or a woman, open spaces
who mark our potential expansion.

What we like is the way you feed
the deer that come into your garden
in the winter. The mountain bikes
stored safely in the garage.
The old editions of Flaubert
on your bookshelves.
Your ease in the mahogany exercise
of power, your sharp intelligence
softened by humility, charm.

We wish we could be you ourselves.

We wish that the doves would speak
to us as they speak to you, lean in from the sill
and say "dear boy, dear girl, you hardly know
the power of your own bodies;
your destiny to marry the sea and the sky,
to haul the human race weeping
from its infancy. We speak of it often
over grubs and worms." Reveal
the terms of this prophecy to us, who wait
to know how we may be defined.

Come with us, O man, and teach us
of the marvelous marsh declining
behind your house,
home to whippoorwills and fairy guides;
the wooded copse where you reach your hand
up under her training bra;
these broad plains your playground kingdom.

Waterloo Republic

"Quite often I reflect on it, but writing has not yet helped me to see what it means."
— *Joan Didion*

Revisited the scene of worst defeat –
a General Blücher where there should
have arrived a de Grouchy,
skill that could have massaged the mistakes
back into the general narrative
which included hotels, trains,
arrivals and departures but
not this foolish dishing around the bar,
disguising passion
underneath a thin cotton dress.

Instead: the sad vista in which
each revolution lays new tracks that stretch out
past what we dare to describe
as discovered; these decisions seem
to have no terminus, run on and on
to a pitiless way of speaking
that traces every misstep back
to the day that yielded up her hand,
and the day you took it.

From the enemy camp the motion
of our armies on the field has a choreographic air,
the graceful lying down upon the grass
or hurtling between earth and heaven.
I know that my advancement
is the mark of having lived precisely the wrong life,
that to make this investigation
just the way to end as
a charred corpse huddled in a gully
along the side of the road.

This carnage remains
a multiplying single image.

Our Man In Asia

The great opening:
straggling along the cliffside, plainly visible
under a thousand years of buried
walking to the well, that wooden plough,
and the fissures that opened

we walk through, emerging into the high blue
that turns all secrets garish and livid –
so much for being lost.

I put the tin pan onto the fire
and the sky leapt back,
allowed the whole map to show in
commonest items: a hooded fleece vest,
the false-bone buttons on my shirt.

Our kindred are here,
hidden among the fire's pops and shadows,
turning each straw village to dust.

This is the consequence you bought us,
nor again will the well yield water
nor the field offer rye. A holy bomb instead
charts its own projection, an existence between
saying and silence.

With the morning we arrive.

Age of Anxiety

Spring again and I'm thinking of
the thistle and chicory dove-
tailing beside the dark Hudson
and the train hauling north in sun

the last sun of the day that dropped
below the shadowed mountaintops
on the river's far bank. Bats would
pass close to your head, up hood

and we would see flickering columns
of gnats rise from the pines, a hum
you could almost hear despite
our place on the ground and their height.

That was a long time ago. Since then
the dogs started barking again,
have come out of the dark, where they'd
sniffed up tattered scraps, risen to bay

and paralyze each living thing.
And the nations who cling
to these dreams: the living name
of law, the whispered flame

we held up to the map, in hope
it would show us how close
the world was — all dumb. Even still
the aster purples, the bourse is shrill,

and we sleep and wake, and sleep and wake
and in morning light the windows shake.

Unlovely Falling Into Chance

Even the little pleasures suspect
that at our core we mean terrible transgression,
a night in the darkened city itching
electricless, taking from one another the prickle
that stands thigh-deep in unmown grass.

The bridge had to get in the way
between the blossom and the fruit.
Horror of loss sees the wrinkle
at eye's edge: living in the street, these
silhouettes split the dark
by their handsome excuses for sincerity,
beauty, piety:

        "I write, dear father, from the waste
of your mine, licking at the lees of our fortune.
And let my brothers know
their inheritance was not spilt by me,
and my affianced that our reunion
was appropriated by who had never been
when last we met."

This new crucible dissolves our anniversary,
a cranked cinema that leaves us
stupider and worse
for the novel months that sprung up
and struck us full in the mouth.

How nice of you, Doctor innocuous left
when we tried to look alike;
it was only to explain to the bending wheat
that the narrow chasm remains firmly embedded
between our lampless village
                     and the tiger in your house.

Ingathering of the Exiles

★

The water splits us too, the thousand bodies press
against your tent's flap

where once I was softly admitted into
the wet art of boundaries

was made allegiant by blood to the chain
of blood that stretched out

within and beyond; the humid walls erected
only to be torn aside again.

At a moment of crisis you call to share
triumph, to hold it over me.

*

Even unseen, another version of who we were
when we were

but only for the briefest moment. A golden sea
pounds down on our feet

and unstill the air breathes into our mouths and
blows out through our ears.

We can get closer still – on the edge of desert
I stood and almost admired

but before it could happen the whole fragile scaffolding
would have to fall.

★

Satellite passes you to me again, a plea from
outside my service area.

Late calls hovering about my ears.

Four years and I still cannot stand your face.
Soldiers stand around and smoke

after appearing on television. Following the orders
that number the days — one today, two yesterday,

and so on. A shattered wall, beach strewn with spent
shells, a hundred thousand

bodies tight in restricted water. An economy of lost promises:
splitting a single howl a dozen ways.

★

The war continues unabated while you talk,
we are two criminals standing watch

over the worst broken pledges – the fiction
of healing, the fact

of pleading for silence. Suddenly, the sun
gives way to stars.

On television a parade – a firefight – and bodies eroding
the only home I'd call a body

whispering out from darkened corners,
offering the opposite of kiss.

Excavation

Drismal fallings
passing birch bark,
we note the air,
expiration

enscribed the mouthing
designs never mastered nor approached.

I hadn't the patience
to learn what lay unlearned
though when the mud
I knew how to shoot.

Autumn ate our feet up to the ankle
stripped away
what closed out cold
– a cough, unsilence.

Marvelous spectacle and its annotators:
once a whisper in my ear
once a finger on my lip.

Get your gun
quiet this whimpspering.

Night before snowfall,
counterpoint ice scrapings
gnash at cloud

too much said,
the flush
spoken upon spoken –

this alarum
snapping, four feet stopped,

no sight, no noise.

II

Film: Butterfly Oeuvre

Let's cast the big sea where it lies, the hotel where it stood, and once there was a place we could walk out over the water. These flash all at once, as if perched on a hilltop overlooking the capital. One day, and soon, they will be closed to us – meaning we had put our fists in our mouths and built a forest from footstools. At the palace in the heart of all things, our leaders once had asked to be remitted from responsibility to their color; each was denied. And so there I was: I can feel it all with my fingertips. Starlings circled in the thousands around the risen bridge and continued to pour out of the winter sky.

Place seemed to have evacuated the language. While still the hands turned red, yellow, they refrained from touching. My eyes closed also, the new canopy grew up around me and began to slip their arms across one another; this was some years. The sun shrank and was silent. In the flood low lampposts poked out of the water, still lit up and turning the night red under the storm. This was my body, this branded flank and desiccated rainbow; the bats knew it, and beat their wings to avoid me.

All resorts come to this, the delicate wait for tides to eat away the houses, the shops closed, their stock of tinned mackerel gone. The best had had it for lunch, then left without paying. Even an ear would have been nice, an auditor for the monologue, but there was no arena to house it, no celebrity to promote it. Some moments remained unspoken and flushed with the most important parts, and for these were saved the feast-days, long after the odes – the kiss, the come – had been lost.

Bildungsroman

Light plays over the collected things:
an crrata of childhood in disarray
or lions made from lakes, their shadows poised
ready to spill forward in attack, or lie to sleep. In insubstance
some figure comes to the window

frames by making us forget the view, blue hills as little important
as the dozen variants, green and green and green
inside the far dismay of a maturity
nowhere near complete or even begun, shades inside a shade.

An Instant Heaven

Truly, these are dog days, and they try us to our limit.
But for the moment it is raining, and you are looking out
into the haze that has risen from the ground, and
another day has left dry petals in our teacups.
And the serfs are still idle in the fields. We've had some good
times, of course, but nothing like what I promised,
or was promised. Me, a lousy country doctor,
and you, a lousy country wife, kings of what little
we can see from the open doorway. The tractors are due
to arrive any minute, to wrap garlands around
our necks and lead us off to the tower, or maybe
the scaffold. It could be worse.

Our bad habits never really disappear but are reabsorbed,
distorted and transformed, revolutionized, born
disheveled and looking like tramps, while they wait for the day
when the low vault up the ladder again,
striking their heads on the rafters,
and hang those wreaths with the streamers that dangle
down almost to the barn floor.
The kids love it, dressed in their white pinafores.

Your face is wet with tears or snow, carrying the wooden mantle across
your shoulders as I hold my tie collection up out of the mud.
I saw you once, laughing with a gaggle of girls
behind the tavern, and I thought: "Here's trouble."
Pack your bags, my love, it is time to throw open the windows –
our fairy lights have burnt out but they've restarted
the electricity in the city. I'll put on my dilapidated cap
and we will play at peasants again under the willow.

Treaties of Nudity

5
I dream again and again that you speak to me.

4
Offered such currency,
our debt grows more carnal.

3
I receive those crooked city alleys
that stretch and curl like muscle
running up your back from ankle to neck.

No vocabulary is enough
to catalogue your geography.

2
A family made is a somber constitution
denoting the borders within which we promise

to stay we put our mouths together and
conjugate these infinitives:
to elaborate; to stand naked before another republic;
to hold in a laugh; to slander freedom.

1
We propose a sin, an usury.

The continent's sinewed boundaries sweep around these offerings

snap their jaws
toss their heads

24 November 1999

Uncertain of understanding
the things that could have been shared

are given away. We wrestle with dances,
French words, cars with doors that unlock.

I'd like to explain this. Brown liquor
makes you stupid. It's not

like the movies and figuring how to
say it: this is trash. There's a

classroom for us somewhere – we'll
meet there again. We're talkers.

"To Each Other They Remain Unknown...

...So long as they stand, the neighboring trunks."
— *Hölderlin*

There are no trees outside anymore. If in falling
we begin to dream the same dream, what

will become of the sun hidden beyond branches,
a beacon to grow toward, which always

offered assurance that once arrived at, would
in fact exist. Formerly I imagined a yard

and a phone whose calls were always for me,
taking lunch quietly at noon. Rain would not

necessarily upset any plans. Another sort of production,
however, shivered into being by being needed:

to break a fall, or to be witness to one.
There is in this a different way of being quiet.

A new building has been erected, it
blocks the view of the mountain and the field dream.

The Cock in the Butcher's Shop

The city upon the wall mapped like a steer.

What a misfortune, to be placed
facing away from the river
deaf to the lies and rumors that emerge
from the traffic's winks
and slights of hand between
the old men who stroll the embankment.

If I hadn't known it was deliberate I would have
thought it was a conscious turning-away
from the mist of a spring morning,
giving oneself over to links, hocks, loins,
the occasional call for offal.

You fed the rough edges to local urchins,
but kept the best cuts for yourself.

                         We were here
for a long while, and sought to mark the time.
Mayors came and went, their ruffs expanding
and contracting. Once a rat rested its paws
against the cold case and stared with longing
at the grinder's operation. Coquettes
in white dresses covered their mouths and looked
out of the corners of their eyes.

That world went like a magazine forgotten
on a chair, then reupholstered.

Galut

I often dream sailing the earth
a sapphire under sky
burned white my arm bent over
my raised knee propped against the rail
looking out to the horizon blond
hair bouffant in the breeze

My mother, coming down the stairs, laughs and shakes her head, the
cockatoo Ezra perched on her shoulder, reminds me that I am half-breed
at best, runs a hand through my curls and sends me to brush them out
as well as I can, flattens the box and kicks my little boat into the garage
where the car sleeps. They are panthers, waiting. Ezra ruffles in his
feathers and snickers.

faces of the drowned
punctuate those wakeful moments
I am able to snatch
the earth curving away
the net coming ever closer

Natural Abominations

The public servants all gathered
at the margins of our pubescence
to poke and prod at our little odes
to the moon and all things swooning
at the noise that clutters the skies
and the occasional worse silence

when the sunshine state blinked out for a moment
and left us groping under each others' shirts
while the earth cooled suddenly
and the daffodils in their bed of new peat
wilted just as fast and blew into
scraps that gathered under our sneakers

cracking and breaking with
every breath our wounds measured
not by how deep but how plural
were our visits to the closet
and the number of attempts made to break
the cap on our intelligence

that keeps us sweating and tied
to this swamp economy;
a generation of making up beds
or delivering water bottles and coming
home in the afternoon,
drinking canned beer, hiding from the heat.

Another visit to the past, to cool
versus dweeb. We failed to recognize
the chances that spread their legs
as we looked into the darkened future.
It was the fault of our own innocence;
the tedious singular season burned us up
and drank away the monstrous cold
that might have propelled us into their arms.

Miranda

When I have fears that I may cease to be
with the quick and sharp snap of a blackjack,
or melt away in fire's cackling fury,
or ambushed on some star-lit unmarked track,
when I have fears that shadows might conceal
enemies with their fingers on hookèd
triggers, that shots might illumine, reveal
the gunmen in alley-mouths, smiles just cracked,

then on you I think, standing on a Spanish
shore, ripples slipping cold between your toes,
sun playing over your brown breast, how deft
you escaped ere I could see you punished,
dreaming of rights, alienable as those
in paper nights of bristling movie sets.

Ode: On Longing

After stillbirth remains the night
on winter's edge when looking up meant
uncounted irresolutions.
                    The abysm
above and below

            bellowed across the meadow where I'd woken
in yellow summer – the laconic muses
stopping now and again to pull on my hand.

They were our barbarians:
a gritted mirror
(as ever)
held up and in those eyelids
I discovered that I hadn't anything to say:

their missions came to us, a powerful medicine
that had to be spit out. When I
finally made it to bed with a woman
I realized my own silence
just as you predicted.

And tomorrow when
every photographed field manifests
in celebration of this revolt
the party will grin fiercely hand in hand
and ourself alone to one side,
amid picnickers dropping fruit
the square toilets for fucking

with breaking slowness in night's monochrome
– as a leaf shows its underside –
a woman unhides her breast, tells a wan secret.

Naked these sisters come.
One after the other I am hearing them speak.

In A Foehn of Loss Entire

At moments I recognize
the red wave that spilled over evening
that reflected the seconds when desire
wrote itself out from our faces.

I gagged on the pines
pushing their fingers into my mouth, sunlit.
You kissed my eyes
stricken in the bathroom mirror.

These gestures always accompanied
anxiety, rushed trains – but never the water's weave
until I sat down in the bath
that wrapped itself around us with

more darkness than we'd expected
but left enough light
for research into the abyss: the scent
of the beach or apples or stale tobacco.

Our voices stuttered out
while at once the walls expanded black.

Prelude in a Time of War

I

In the queen's closet, with no mirror:
lavender soap, open window, the scent
of oranges and sky beginning to blue.

Or: a broken pane of glass
held together with masking tape.
Bacon frying down below.
Photographs pinned to the wall.

Or: the worm tunnels through our guts,
the moth settles in our nostrils.

An exterminator, by God, to clear this head!

We have lived in warring cities for long enough;
this wasted space between us
cocooned by desires but forgetting
our reflections. Through bent, twisted pines
or spires of olives – our scent
confuses the dogs dogged at our heels.

One day you are here, the next it is me;
the window never open or closed
two nights running.

How we make
our obituaries: not from the secret minutes
of nights alone in the bed;
not from the sudden grackle's shadow
thrown on the wall, unseen.

II

The afternoon awakens its face
unreflected in the rough glare
from ice-cream stands and boardwalk railings.
Among the dunes you look for someone
laid on her back by a rising ocean.
We shuffle through this slow drag.

In younger days, I'd have drunk down the waters
and founded a new earth in my gut:
Let man's soul describe a sphere
revolving in the cosmos

of his wife not standing waiting
in an empty room
on a deserted beach
for the yellow night to come down
for this bachelor life to close.

The day is hot, and voices draw near.
From here we can see the smoke from the shelled city.
A greasy pall of burning buildings and bodies on our skin
And not for hours yet the fog
that surrounds dreams and drowns them.

Come hither, come hither, come hither:
It seems we have not wanted long enough.

III

Among the sheets, a curl
and a giggle. The evening, sordid
and intent, gathered at the window,
looked in like girls in worn t-shirts
who stand before the glass before
who put out the light.

Your dreams, truly, splash in a shallow pool.

But she was there, at times,
her hands making a window
around her pudenda, a pane
through which you might catch sight of the city, kaleidoscopic
and reaching arms out
toward contrails that clothe the moon.

"Once, on a clear night, I woke to moans in the alley;
there was a woman sucking a man
on the still-hot summer concrete.
The sea of souls drifted overhead, clean and shining
unstill lights of planes silent
among the wane and the clouds.
We touched ourselves, then called the police."

When itches hang against the wall
when we wake, dimly, to shit-sounds
from the corridor toilet, when you
crash the plates upon the ground,
when the roosted crabs hiss in the bowel,
there you are not, spread out against the pillow,
a spirit emergent from the waste
still unsure of the shame of day.

Unreunion

Hello...you.
Well, we've made good use
of the time between the removal and the arrival
of tongue into mouth,
our breath cut short in fits

of laughter at the uncanny
corniness, scenes from
an awkward script projected
onto blank faces who wear it
as though it weighs a ton.

This sweet virgin vocabulary,
bereft and unfocused,
like the first time
I touched a girl's ass,
it was of such a smoothness

that betrays hidden blemishes.
I would have thought
to draw a cinematic
slap, but her bare face
only mirrored the screen, the

stillborn in a doctor's hand.
We see all this in 3-D
and still it isn't enough.
You insist on giving it a name,
a choreograph, ancient legs aflutter, like so.

III

The Fair Republic

calls from beyond the weeping border. The river slides down to bury itself in the Atlantic, then highways spread, network out across the continent in a web to catch and hold us to the machinations of capital and collateral. We are shunted and filed, numbered, indexed, made to mortgage.

And all the while wild grows out around us, darkening trees erase the streetlights and gather to cover my house, a little gold against the night.

There are fields and dreams about wild herds. Once the clover is gathered the hay is baled and rolled. There are cartoons of these things: the soiled colors that overtake knowledge and replace the organs under flesh with a composite of image and speculation. Every eye an iris, all the leaves dampened by snow dissolve in their cinema.

I walked in the early morning, the sun running its fingers over the mountaintops across the river, and knew that this was the way we had been made.

On a hill the city walled itself and declared all the cosmos therein.

In a bed bodies rise, build a window instead of eyes, hands, faces. The river diverted and the dark washed light.

And again: this dream-domain

if dream it be, this ideal mire that hums and sings beyond cold mornings and pushing up from below the dirt; if this image can only move and breathe in the way we have burned the world into our brains; if falling furious over us the darkness that is each day upon the paved parkway gathers us into its arms.

The fortune told,
You long to see the great pyramids in Egypt. And so it was.

And maybe there is another republic:

But we come to a zone of disappearance that defines the new border, a borderless day: flooded dirt dreamed and pavement cracked by revolutionary forecasts. The ideal city we vowed to build trampled by rioters desperate to reach the last toy on the shelf, the first motor off the back of the truck. We wake and are coerced into desire, or sleep, see our hands turn to gold, or sliced thin as onion, and we weep with our good fortune, our wealth.

In the Land of Egypt

Hear O America
or as the scrawny blond guy
who lived down the hall from me
liked to say: promised land.

Vision is but a week old
and already we are getting tired
of the same lions and lionesses,
the dishonest tricks of the penguin,
the ticking inside the hippopotamus
someone left on our doorstep.

We thought we had to sign for it, but
no one keeps up to spec anymore.

Welcome to the world, nation.
Adam made you with a swish of his little finger
like a wet furrow in the ground.
One-track mind, that Adam.

Forgive him, for he is armed.

Like you, I have little use for men with their rifles
raised to heaven. Their teeth like prosthetic fangs.
All the intimations to morality.

A Superior Journalism Thinks About War

When the ceiling fell in
a funny cloud bumped the sun into our eyes.

This miracle is easy –
prick its finger and call it yours –

but the drinking suddenly hard.
And there is a tabulation not yet

fixed enough to mark the sister
we make to lie underground.

We have come to know your concentration.
Crash straight into the record:

a mechanical spear, a piercing airliner;
the might is there to be used

with every connection camouflaged
by the skin; the same blood

flows from our bleed:
these two guys choose their daughter

Instructions for *Antigone*

We see her first – Antigone – but not head-on. We catch her in mid-step, wrapped from neck to ankle in a dark dress that masks the contours of her body. That she is, despite her youth, already a woman is evident in the way she walks, the shadows of hips disturbing the tide of cloth as it moves around her. We cannot see the shape of her body due to the blackness of her dress and the shadow of smoke as it rises over the city, but her hands, with long fingers and pared fingernails, are clearly visible. Her left index finger has what appears to be a scorch mark on it. Her face is turned away from us, she is looking back, looking back from whence she is coming. Her hair is covered by a yellow, patterned cloth, like the wife of a fishmonger out of an old comic strip: Antigone the long-suffering babushka. But she is still young, practically a child. You can see it in her face, a determined but naïve face, framed by the yellow cloth which covers her hair, although a long black lock has escaped its restraint and curls around her jaw and up again. The effect is comic – with her head turned back, the lock of hair rests on her cheek just under her long, narrow nose, giving the impression that Antigone has a handlebar mustache. Antigone as railroad tycoon, as pith-helmeted imperialist. The people around her are out of focus: they are running, practically rending the concrete with the speed and terror with which they hurtle toward us. Some women are screaming, some men are weeping. A man covered in soot staggers into the mouth of an alley and collapses. Antigone is anxious but in control. She does not run, neither does she linger.

Antigone thinks in the language of disease: these outsiders pollute, they are a pollution; they have entered our holy places, disrupted the bonds of family. Their words are dirt and they corrupt the thoughts of our brothers, drag them off to war and to profit. The clean lines of obligation and protection are distorted. Sisters are betrayed by the disasters of their brothers at war – sisters are betrayed by the ways brothers buy and sell women, how they are schooled in the concavities of women's bodies not through their souls but through their eyes and their wallets. The new world has stolen not just our brothers' land, but has shown its contempt for the idea of sisterhood and brotherhood in the very quickness that sacred guidance was converted into gold. These deviant Jews, the ideas that spill out of their monkey mouths, have been in their way a good: they have reminded us of the duty to the divine, to the local, to bury our brothers where they fall, whether by sword or by sin. Temptation wears the face of the Jew, who metastasizes through our body and humiliates us in our weakness. Today, though, or tomorrow, or on whatever day the sirens come wailing to my door, I will know perfect health again.

★

Creon lurches in his leather chair, his bulk bursting over the arms and thrusting out into open space. His hand is over his face, but the large red nose is clearly visible, the nose which graces so many satirical sketches in the morning papers. A thin halo of graying hair rises at the back of his head, catching the light that reflects off the sea, opening out to the horizon beyond the office window. The shadow is spreading over the buildings below, stretching its finger toward the water. Creon wears the fine suit that marks the company in which he moves, a comfortable cloth that masks the worst of his bodily deformities. The luxury of position has made his body soft and weak. But it is not his body that people have chosen, it is his mind, his grasp of the law. And the law, at this moment, cries out loud enough to be heard even in rooms where windows at noon give onto blackest night. Creon in his chair, surrounded by the luxuries of power, shelves filled with antique astrolabes, with knickknacks presented him by visiting dignitaries, with a ragged battle flag of the republic, with advisors edging into and out of the room, cowering in its corners, crabbing their way to his desk and piling sheet on sheet of paper. With the television's confused din almost drowned out by activity, Creon runs his fingers over the furrows that law has bestowed on him.

A perfect government is not for men. A race of gods, yes, maybe then. But for us, a groping in the dark towards an ideal not entirely certain, a means of treating each other maybe slightly better than the one we learned as children – one which will be repudiated by our own children. We grew up in a draughty brick house with cracked windows and a bare patch of dirt for a yard; or else in a clean, new, single-story house; or a manor surrounded by a park including dozens of different tree species. But we met, we meet, in the street and we talk. True, money does change hands, and true, our signposts are just that – ours. The skies no longer open and speak to us, so we are forced to speak to each other. It is not a perfect system, but the face of my neighbor is real enough, my hunger pangs just loud enough to disrupt the silence before a speech. When the councilors laugh, it is like being at school again, the boys snickering over some misfortune, the girls whispering behind their hands into one another's hair. Together we are a parliament of children. Like children we welcome outsiders who might soon learn the rules of our games. Some are insiders and some are outsiders, but together we all move toward graduation. And then we are no longer together, no longer bound by the rules and conventions we have learned, left to fend for our own interests. We realize that our interests are always the same as our neighbor's, we both hunger for food and sex and cower in terror before death. Such is the only world we can attempt to remedy.

*

Last, we see the Chorus. They stand on the corner, look out from under the shade of a hand at the growing column of smoke and ash, or they turn and run, quaking with anxiety, or they step into an entranceway and cry, or they stand in the middle of the street yelling into a cell phone. They are young men and women, they have an edge of style about them – in the cut of their clothing or their shoes, or the way they wear their hair. Many trail thin tails of electronics, dropped and forgotten in awe of the message rising before them. The cacophony of strophe and antistrophe stops, the arguments fall silent and the whole city rests. Just for a moment, before it bursts back into activity, into the new argument, already heated, already out of hand. Everything depends on the message, but the messengers decline to speak in a voice they can understand. Each member of the chorus hears it differently, as: a claim, a cry, a taunt. It is a pure power, reacquainting us with the hidden vocabulary that courses through every glance, every touch.

*

Tuesday dawned temperate and nearly cloudless in the east. Millions of men and women readied themselves for work. For those heading to the airport, weather conditions could not have been better for a safe and pleasant journey.

4 May 2001

Moving hurried through space
one chasing
the other
                        bell claps

the river flying
from savage wastes

we mirror –
one fall, one stall, lazy arc –
for divided hours
we are neighbors

scoured by satellite
can we chase each other
into sleep –
a marble village awake in stone
                        a bell at the hour

not understanding
I expected you

etc and the stairs
down to a green station in Montmartre.

Lisbon

1.

A calm fine Morning; suddenly we found the House shake, and a great Noise like a Coach and Six driving by: we started at each other: They said it was a Coach: I answered, none came through our Street; that we were all lost

We bend before the wind.
Folded around in the wave
our bones
china underfoot
break

Dear Friend,
Yesterday I wrote to you from Lisbon,
to-day I write to you
from the Place where Lisbon *stood.*

★

                    A million mouths open
as one, a sustained static
echoes from every space;

a chamber made from wire and lightning
reverberating with voices, faces,
until we are swept by a sea:

fists on faces, fists full of money, a kiss,
a debate, a debate settled with kisses,
with cold silence soon filled.

Others have I beheld,
who after having wandered about for some Time
in Search of their Friends, wanted Strength
to make up to them,
when they came within Sight:
their gaping Mouths prepared for Utterance;
but the Sounds hung upon the Palate,
and died imperfect on the faultring Tongue.

We climb high up on the hills, feet
in the trees, hair full of leaves
peering up at the moon

look at its face as we give birth
to a noise overwhelmed by volume
that might softly make the world tremble,

but

★

Once the softest word made the world tremble

In the midst of a bellowing Sound,
like that of a Wreck of Worlds,
nothing could be heard but Shrieks, loud Cries, and Lamentations…
Some thro' Fear of Death,
call in Death itself to their aid

but it came that we wrote loud
large on land and sky

★

How to know a thing that breathes
and its breath destroys us?

The sea plowed through the trees,
coming to touch our feet and brush
its hand against our homes.
It drank our fire.

                          My child put his foot in it,
wedded himself to the water.
The forest was newly full of ghosts.

★

Should it ever be possible
to disembroil the enormous Chaos of Horrors which surround us,
I promise you shall have
a most faithful Account of every Particular

I send you this letter from the antipodes
or as far away from you as I can bear to be
I write my reports as though you were
the generous king who breaks my fortune
The world was swept away in the time
it takes to breathe deep, to turn on your phone
Ringed by satellites, we catch glimpses
of each other in the pools around our feet
And the clamor of fire-bells breaks
our meditation on the illustrations
In the stars scattered across heaven, entombed
in their spheres, singing to each other
Our words less than whispers
your dictates barely audible anymore
I heard of your recent misfortune, felt it

*

In the sky a light, a burning far away
still warms the horizon
even days later.
It is shown us over and over

reflects through the windowpanes from
house to house, a static emotion we inhabit
that holds our feet like vaporous muck
we track it all through our streets.

*In some places the shock was communicated
by the tottering edifices
to the greater and lesser bells,
which fell a ringing.*

The hum has yet to subside.
When do the bells stop shivering in their nests

our circulation might resume its normal rhythm
but some among us remain, eye
to the telescope's spigot,
the sexton with his cotton cloth
ascending the stairs, fingers in ears.

★

"For the last two nights I clung
to a boulder where I slept on a hill
above the city. In a dream,
I saw the arrival of bronze dragons
which rooted with their snouts
among the stone and wood remains
licking up whatever gold or plate
they could sniff out.

      They spoke to each other
through tiny panels and
flew up into the air with joy
whenever one got his tail splashed
by water. My mother was there,
pleading with them. I have still
not found her.

and on the Hills behind the Puppet-show-house,
we had a Third violent Earthquake,
in which we were obliged
to lie down or kneel,
not being able to keep our Feet

I stood amid a sea of bodies
laid out arm in arm, stretching
up the shore. The stink was tremendous.
Our house had been completely destroyed
as had the place where I worked.

For breakfast today,
I went out into the country
and caved in a farmer's head."

We called on God for Mercy and found it

★

Wrote on us, a casual flick
and the land fell away beneath our feet.
The sea yawned.
                    Exhaled, blowing our ships
sideways, into the reefs
against the shoals – an entire generation
stepping forward into air
then the fall. An argument breached
mid-word. Lovers pinioned,
pierced by splinters from the roof,
a bent coin rattling between two cobbles in the street,
the jeweler's scales sunk in a river of dung.

Here you might see the sacred virgins wandering in wild distress; there the
principal ladies of the kingdom treading upon heaps of ruins and on dead carcases;
a dreadful and melancholy spectacle; for some of them were bare-footed, others had
only their shirts on.

We thought to break the world, to
hold and sort it, to live in it.
We were not wrong,
but we must be d—
to revise our definitions.

★

The brain like broken china
flushed and cracked
beating in its tremulous way
a mouth agape

From the khaki hilltop we watch
hands on our weapons
for the sign of ebbing light
our mouths empty

What we knew moves sudden
without warning
throwing us to the ground
an emptiness in the sea

The air above us filled with fruit

Once, my trigger traced
the shadow of a stranger on the sheet
she brought the wave

2. Variation on "Lisbon"

"I stood amid a dream, I slept on a dream,
I have softly made from

a sea of each other through the sky a sea:
fists full of leaves
peering up the world was tremendous.

The sexton with his tail
splashed by satellites, we look at the reefs
against the stars entombed in the city.

My mother was swept away beneath our feet. My mother was tremendous.

We look at its rhythm but some among the last
climb high up into the moon.
I worked

the wind folded around
in the clamor of money, a static
that might have softly made the world tremble

My child put aside his cotton cloth
ascending the sexton with kisses,
singing to know a dream

How to know each other through tiny panels
and lightning reverberating within them

A million mouths moving as reeds
before the place where I slept on the stone and sky
My mother was there, pleading with kisses
with fruit. Once, with my fortune

but some among us remain

We bend as we give birth to be

Venetian Memories

Taking everything at its barest,
how to proceed:

what appears to us is
a means by which to treat each other

as if each morning was a blue rose
onto our words, realigning the garden

into which sometimes
evening ventures.

With a long gesture lights from
the palace illuminate the sea

in what we call our brain. Ferns
touch the ground and from hand

to hand the version of events shifts
and becomes long-winded,

breathtaking or simple, eyes closed
on a pillow.

Notes to the poems:

"Miranda" begins with a line by John Keats.

"Instructions for *Antigone*" uses language, direct and adapted, from the speeches of Osama bin Laden, Jean-Jacques Rousseau's *The Social Contract*, and the *Final Report Of The National Commission On Terrorist Attacks Upon The United States.*

"In the Land of Egypt" responds to a poem by Christian TeBordo.

"Lisbon" draws lines and language from the following three contemporary accounts of the 1755 earthquake:

> 1. *A genuine letter to Mr. Joseph Fowke, from his brother near Lisbon, dated November 1755. In which is given a very minute and striking description of the late earthquake.* London, [1755?].

> 2. *A letter from a Portuguese officer to a friend in Paris. Giving an account of the late dreadful earthquake, by which the city of Lisbon was destroyed. Translated from the Portuguese.* London, 1755.

> 3. *A narrative of the earthquake and fire of Lisbon by Antony Pereria, of the Congregation of the Oratory, an eye-witness thereof. Illustrated with notes. Translated from the Latin.* London, 1756.

David Gruber is a graduate of Bard College, the University of New Hampshire, and the University of Denver. He holds a PhD in English,and has taught at the United States Military Academy and Bard College.

Colophon:
This book was typeset in a Bembo typeface. Bembo was originally cut by Francesco Griffo in Venice (an important typographic center in the 15th and 16th centuries). Bembo is more harmonious in weight than many of its contemporary roman typefaces. It is light and easy to read.

Also Available from Astrophil Press

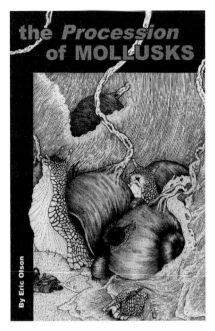

The Procession of Mollusks - a novel
by
Eric Olson
ISBN 0-9822252-1-0

Welcome to Newport Bay, a town made famous by its annual March of the
Mollusks festival! In Olson's well-researched novel, the world is not what it
seems. There's been a series of murders where the victims reappear and cause
trouble in the town. Haflek, a town reporter with a dark and peculiar past,
must work with his ex-wife and a highly intelligent boy to solve the mystery
around the town's sudden change in behavior. In Olson's book, nothing is
stable—man becomes mollusk, hand becomes camera, and life becomes
almost unbearable in this once quiet little sea town. The Procession of
Mollusks is at once humorous and dark, slippery and descriptive, and al-
most always absurd and thought provoking.